I Loved You Once

Bee DeMarco

BookLeaf Publishing

India | USA | UK

Presentation by *BookLeaf Publishing*

Web: www.bookleafpub.com

E-mail: info@bookleafpub.com

ISBN: 9789358318289

First edition 2024

DEDICATION

To Skylar,

How I wish I could share my pride with you now.

To the life we planned

To Joeii,

My honest soulmate,

Wishes of your complete happiness

ACKNOWLEDGEMENT

I would love to thank so many things for inspiring these words, these feelings and stories. I think most of all I would like to thank Skylar G.S. for inspiring these poems the most. I would love to thank my siblings as well as they had a huge hand in my progress as a writer.

I would also like to express my gratitude to my two favorite teachers, Mrs. Chassereau and Mrs. Klein who helped me through a lot of the times I was struggling with my inspiration. I will get you two a copy of this book as a remembrance and a promise to use everything you taught me.

To my siblings, being as chaotic as they are, teaching me to write under pressure. They gave me the best babysitting job I could ever do.

Another thing about me is I always honor my promises, Joeii, thank you. For everything, the world would be bleak without you. In this collection I have a few poems dedicated to my time with you.

In The Rain

That feeling that comes with storms,
I never understood.

My emotions and expectations change with the
wind,
The rain is a therapist.

That feeling that pulls you into the past,
isn't real to me.

Instead of caring for myself,
I danced with the spirits of the wind.

That feeling is more I can say,
Real to everything I own.

My world changes with the rain,
It pulls me with the wave of time.

That feeling that comes with storms?
I finally understand.

Only when I saw them play within the gift of
rain,
Did I understand.
The feeling that comes with the rain,

It changes in association.

I never saw the rain as an entity,
Now I see it as I see the wind.

It is the messenger of a recovering echo,
The echo of the past.

The rain is cyclic,
Just as the path of healing.

The rain is a messenger,
A messenger of recuperation.

Idolize

Oh, how I idolize you,
Characters from fantasy worlds built upon time,
Changes in the wind,
The planets and the stars.
Oh, how I wish you were real,
I doused myself in lighter fluid,
Covered in the scars I feel from you,
Though I'm slightly glad I didn't die that night.
Oh, how I love you,
Your music tearing me apart,
Your voices pulling me in as a God,
Telling me things about myself I never knew.
Oh, how I beg for you,
I beg for your voices,
I beg for your skin,
I beg to be you.
Oh, how I wish to be created,
How I wish to be drawn,
How I wish to be real,
How I wish to be you.

Oh, how I wish I were a character,
Someone you can draw,
Someone you can change,
Someone to unravel.

Oh, how I wish I were yarn,
Red like the blood oozing down my legs,
Red like the blood I used in my hair,
Red like the drops on my shirt.
Oh, how I wish I were like you,
I took every dollar from my name,
I'm giving it to you, my love.
Every dollar, every cent, hours of my sleep.
Oh,
How I idolize you,
Oh,
How I idolize you.

Change in the Wind

I felt your energy change towards me,
Was that a lie you told yourself,
Thinking that it would make me happy,
When all I wanted was you?

I loved you as the wind loved the sea.
But then I changed,
I grew,
And we were separated by a hurricane.

It's as if the wind knew,
The wind is an accomplice to the sea,
Can we change the future now?
I hope now you'll see what you broke.

Just a change apart from the master of the wind,
Pull me apart,
Not from the heart of yours,
Help me pull away from the wind.

A change in the wind,
I hear words in lyricless melodies,
Screaming out in pain,
Holding my heart hostage from the messages of
the wind.
Love touching across time,

A pure rage in the heart of the wind,
Caring for a chance to feel the sea,
Wishing they were not one and the same.

Pull me out of here,
I wish I were a syren instead of the mermaid I
was,
Don't hide yourself from me,
I love you.

I love you.

I love you as the wind called,
Mama's boy, mama's boy.

The Weight of Iron

Before I felt you,
I felt the iron in my blood.
Before I realized,
I felt the bite of fire.

You are someone I admire,
Someone that feels connected,
I will learn well from you and pull you close,
I will learn your skills.

Gifted in metal making and fire,
Gifted in technology and weapons,
The colors red and blue tied together,
Stuck with me like loyalty.

Iron is the weight of blood,
You can kill ten thousand men
Only to make a dagger,
I will learn from you.

The thoughts inside my head led me here,
Tell me,
Will we learn to know of each other,
Two sides of different worlds?

We are one with passion,

I will be the writer,
I will tell your stories and bring them to life,
If you will teach me the art of iron.

I will hold our torrid hearts,
Metal roses,
Iron supplements,
If you will teach me the art of iron.

The art of blood,
Vines growing from what we built together,
My god of fire,
Hephaestus.

Sleepless

I lie within the softness of fiber,
Comfort from innocent days.
That is when it hits.

Cold,
Rough,
Broken,
Heavy.

My body shaking and frozen in the fear,
Fear of a dead monster,
A dead monster.
I lie within my own mind,
Waiting for the pain.
That's when it starts,
Bloody,
Scary,
Lost,
Memories.

My body stuck within its own bones,
Fae are trying to pull me out,
For once of protection
I lie stuck in a trance,
Knowing the night will never end.

That is when it all starts,
The memories,
Flashbacks,
Pain,
I remember it all for a moment.

My bones now offered to the fae,
My blood now offered to the Gods,
My spirit now offered to myself.

If Only

If only the words could leave my throat,
Then I would be free.

If only my smile was real,
Then I would be real.

If only the little red lines helped,
Then I'd be long gone.

If only my chance to shine was on stage,
Then I'd be an actor.

If only my body felt like mine,
Then I'd be me
If only I were real,
Then I would be safe.

If only I were dead,
Because this isn't living.

My Earthly Desire

I
I know you
I know you and how I feel
I know you and how I feel about you and I
I don't know how you feel about me.
I wish my earthly desire felt more ethereal,
You were the goddess of my time.
I wish I knew what to say then,
Back when we were kids,
Mumbling our words.

I know you,
I let you try to know me,
You mean the world to me,
A reverse fairytale,
Gifted by a bubble of insecurity,
I love you
I said out of desperation,
But I never stopped loving you.
I made a promise long ago.

In every life we have shared
this promise to you was to love and cherish you
I wake up and watch us both bleed in lives we
have never met,
Tied and torn between strings of fate,

I wrote you letters as we were royalty,
I sung you songs as a bard,
I gave you prophecies as our counterparts,
We have always been one,
Our souls chopped off the same star.

One gifted by the moon, another by Venus.
Blessed in every world we are brought to,
Our digital age completely together yet
separated,
I wish my desire did not exist,
I want everything with you,
We are a fairytale,
Everything started when we said
'I do'

Lady of the Woods

The trees smell of sulfur and ash,
A fear now true,
I'm running from the past,
The sky's fading blue

I'll run until I feel free,
One with the pack of wolves,
For my name is Bee,
Even as far as the moon pulls

I believe I will be saved,
By a man they always asked,
No, by the enslaved
Always afraid of the craft

Following the daughter of the moon,
Through every turn and tree,
Carving into them with any rune,
And suddenly I was three.

Running from the very same man,
Who threatens me today,
Too bad I became the leader of the white wolf
clan,
Forever hunting him as our prey
Protected by the forest,

Protected by My Lady,
Not to be confused with a florist,
Athena, My Lady,

If you hear my thoughts,
See me running from my world,
Take as many arrow shots,
For my blood to pour

Pulled into the mouth of a demon,
Trembling,
Let me be a free man,
Allow me to be the son of the moon

Play Fights

Never have I felt more me than with you,
But never have I felt more afraid.

These games we play,
They are dangerous.

We play and we dance,
Just as we fight and prance.

But we fight with love,
Spray bottle wars of sudden joy.

I know it won't last forever
No matter how hard we try,
This lifetime won't last forever.

Play fighting the days,
Gentle deals with death.

We are one in the same,
Two souls pulled from the experience of
stardust.

Just like our last lifetime,
Just like our last world we built.

I want to build on it,
We can work through it all.

Two halves of a whole bonded together,
Two halves of a whole pulled from the gods.
We will make this lifetime last.

Playing through the fields,
Knowing what comes next.

Whether we are gods,
Or made of stars,
I promise to always play with you.

Fear of abandonment

I feel as though this needs to be said,
However you take it may change,
My words mean what they mean,
But fear is everlasting.

You say you're going to stay,
You say that you love me,
My only motherly figure that I can trust,
But on the gods' will,
Sometimes I fear you will leave.

I may worship the sun and the moon,
But I see the way they push and pull,
We get along,
But for how long?

We had a fight,
I was overly attached to something fake,
No matter how much I apologize,
It feels like you hate me over it,

I know you won't leave,
But my heart doesn't.

The fear is overwhelming to the point where if
you're mad at me,

I'll try to make you leave.

We have most of our lives planned out,
I cannot live that way.

I love you,
I want you to stay,
But I know that if you leave I'll let you go.

I love you,
I hate you,
The things we both went through,
I know we're trying to make it work,
But will it?

I know living together is a big change,
I know it will take a toll,
Will you stay after?

Will you still love me?

My words and thoughts are inconsolable,
My fear of you leaving will always be,
But I am more afraid of what I'll do if you try.

I miss you.

But what if we're nothing more than a fever
dream?

He who Lives

I have always been envious of happy endings,
Reading through lines and lines of ruin,
Lines and lines of running,
Lines and lines of despair.

I have always loved the endings the most,
Following every word like a shark and a bubble,
Following every word hung on the edge,
Following the guesses of their future.

I have been called
'She who follows'
Throughout my lifetime,
This is not my perception.

I am one with the wind,
I am one with the rain,
I have always loved to read,
Adolescence was when I fell in love with
tragedy.

When I found tragedy,
I found war,
I found aggression,
I found me.
But it was the magic in the tragedy,

The magic of the gifted,
The magic of the talented
I am one with these characters,

I am he who lives,
He who breathes,
He who stands for the moon,
He who sleeps with the sun.

I am he who lives,
He who lives through stories told,
He who lives the tragedy of a woman,
I am he who lived it all.

Wings of Odd Creation

Waiting in the wings,
Parting with the idea to create,
Never the plan for a world of my own,
Music, art, stories, games, harmonies.

Blue wonder of the silver rings,
Painting with the ones who degrade,
Pulling apart the pieces of my world to reap
what I have sown
Lost within a melody I never wrote, as karma
means.

The shadow cast upon me, growing under
strings
Carrying the sorrow I carry from fate
Limelight sweetly takes over my mind, holding
what's no longer my own
Carried by a lullaby, the sorrow that only grows
from a world with intention to kill.

Comfort in another Plane

A place no one believes in,
The safety of a world I could never bring to life.

In a world so vibrant and lonely,
Life only beginning to bloom,

Lonely is the world I see I want to watch it
grow,
Bloom from the ashes of a father's failure.

Grow into a plane of safety existence,
Failure to do so will be catastrophic.

The safety of a world I cannot guarantee,
A place everyone lives in.

Listening to things to bring joy after running out
of time,
The pictures with motion no longer breathing,

The story, the comfort, has died,
A perfect person that only exists behind another
scattered brain,

These things let us drown out the extra noise,

Noise that burns.

'Little Kitty all alone without his lady',
And if I could begin to be anything else, I would
try.

I would love like you,
If only I could escape the plane of comfort,

Since this place has never been tried,
We only survive with our own planes that we
create from a heart,

Based on what we see.
Creation of comfort.

Textured Reality

My reality is known to colors and change,
white is malleable,
red is the taste of iron and the feeling of passion,
orange is the sunset with a lover,
yellow is taffy flavored,
green is seeing the grass for the summer skies,
blue is drinking water and feeling real.

my world is so different and poetry is this world
of mine,
Poetry is white,
it's red,
it's spiced,
it's warm,
it's cold,
poetry is everything and nothing,
my, my words they seem to fail,

poetry is this:
it's torn, it's stained,
it spans across 189 countries,

humans have stained it with blood,
tears,
dyes,
ink

the world it seems, the world it changes,
it's being dropped from the sky from a siren,
falling into the arms of a mermaid,
turning a gorgon to stone,
it is becoming a king,
murdering a queen,
falling in love,
poetry is everything... and yet it is nothing.

poetry is red, the color of passion,
poetry is orange, the color of energy
poetry is yellow, the color of joy,
poetry is green, the color of growth,
poetry is blue, the color of loyalty,
poetry is purple, the color of power,
white is every color mixed together.
white is new,
white is real,
white is change,

white is power,
poetry is everything...
and poetry is nothing.

How I Knew

I have always been on every side of anxiety,
Deeply afraid and alone,

I already felt all of this before,
It may not be easy for you,
but it hurts me a lot,

I have been on every side of depression,
Each emotion multiplied to the power of 23,

I already know how this feels,
It is no longer easy,
I'm dancing through the woods praying for a
spike,

This is what I know,
The pain of every word,
Replaying in my head.

A Grave built for More Than One

I see his world crash before me, taken too soon.
Never to be one understanding that breaks the
rope holding onto life.
A single lifeline means so much to one place,
But the grave was made for more than one, more
than two, or even a hundred.

A hundred torn hearts, shredded and bathed in
blood,
A place built for death undiscovered, to hide
away the crime of a single mind,
Life pulling and building a community unwilling
to fight for the safety of themselves.
Soon, the town will burn and fight its way
proceeding through the warning.

Blood dropped from every hidden character
behind a screen,
Minds broken beyond repair, enveloped through
the glass,
Themselves are the only fear of losing,
Warning the next of the pain they endured,
hoping for a listener.

Screen of boxes and pixels,
Glass to cover and burn when it's used.
Losing the fear of being loved by someone far
out of league,
Listener, I beg you to stay, the characters call
for.

Pixels, they burn and cry,
Used for time to make sense,
League of a broken legend,
For the grave is meant for more than one, more
than a hundred.

Spirit of the Vices

A Blue Morpho Butterfly
In love with the Blue-feathered Raven
Though with choices made,
Raven will never survive the pain
Of a wound that Butterfly tried to prevent
A repeated loop of time, one choice can end it
all for their love.

The raven had another love, The Doe.
The Doe was unable to feel the same for fear of
rejection and expression,
The Doe burned her home to the ground with
every step of rage.
Though a man robbed her of her life,
She still led The Morpho Butterfly home,
The Raven never knew how much The Doe did
care.

The Raven has a friend; The Dragon.
The Dragon never knew how enclosed she was
to the Morpho Butterfly,
She hid from this Bay before the storm of time.
The Dragon has a treasure, An empathetic
Canary.
Her lover, Her vice, her survivor.

The Canary is freeing from The Dragon's fear of
ability.

Two sibling wolves, running from their home
out of fear,
A choice for a choice. Younger feeling angry,
abandoned, confused.
They flee the world they knew in order to
survive, meeting little friends on the way.
Crashing in abandoned places, old ancestors, on
their way home.
Never to see the world they left behind in
change.
The older trying to protect its rule, afraid of the
loss they could never see.

What I wouldn't give to see them meet in the bay
for ability,
Gather to explain and share their experiences,
their faults, and magic.
I would give the world to see why every
expression changes and how they bond with
fears,
Butterfly may have lost their ability but their
story changes the others, as they had time.
Canary can feel and see every expressive
change, they'll understand the best.
Little wolf, the ability to move matter as he sees
fit. He can draw illusions out of stones.

When they meet to feel the fear of gray, another
may join their ranks.
Though they may be put into a final grave,
Their lovers and vices will carry on their stories
and tales of freedom,
Watching their buddies grow with the story that
they got to see,
But with every choice, a consequence and a
price.
These are our spirit vices

Magic in Your Eyes

Your eyes,

Blue as the sea,

Whirlpools of thoughts floating by,

Anxious in the present,

Fearing the future.

Your eyes,

Greener in the light,

Suddenly brighter than the sun,

Fiery in the past,

Calmer in the now.

Your eyes,

Grey,

Little as the stones they represent,

Stoic and cold,

Comfort in the rain.

Your eyes,

Hazel mixed,

Everything already baked together,

Soup from the underworld,

Tea from heaven.

Your eyes,

Brown as the chocolate,

Brown as the soft cows in the highlands,

Underrepresented as we have held our light,

Easier to see in the bright sun.

Your eyes,

Black as the night.

Stars glisten across them as thoughts surround,

Given the meaning they believe,

The darkness of the fate that brings us home.

Your eyes,

Red as they stare into mine,

More beautiful than those above,

Gifted as they are and have been,

Show strength and positivity.

Your eyes,

Purple in the light,

Silver in the moon,

Gifted from the wolves you descend,

Show bright promise in our world

Your eyes,

Your eyes,

How I wish to gaze upon them,

How I wish to make them mine,

Your eyes,

The greatest gift you can give

The windows to your soul,

Bear your soul,

Show the inner light,

Your eyes are the thing I love most.

Star-crossed Fate

Two fated hearts melded with desire,
only springing words of fire.

One seen within war,
the other learning to soar.

The boys under laws like no other,
always hiding behind his mother.

They are ones of study and stars,
watching them make tiny scars.

As one drew little red lines,
he ignored every sign.

Waiting on his mother's approval,
but it began only removal.

Fate called for star-crossed lovers.
while pulling them to others.

As they longed for death,
he took a deep breath.

Lost between the worlds,
he has seen his words.

They only fed their guilt,
allowing their daughter to wilt.

Time

The world is surrounded by a miasma,
Forced itself to burn its own creation,
I lay awake around the day,
Forced in the night to breathe it.

Time is of the essence,
Plan plan plan,
Work for the sake of your family,
Work for the sake of supporting us.

Plan Plan Plan,
Work Work Work,
For what?
To enjoy the last years of my life in crippling
pain?
Why should I work hard?

For someone who does not cherish my talents.
Mama said I should succeed if I do.
But she is wrong,
If I don't have fun,
Freedom that we have preached into our hearts,

I'll be lost,
No longer human,
No longer talented.

I want to make mistakes,
So far beyond my pay,
I want to live,
But survival comes first.

Why do I have to be in my 30s before I can live?
I won't be 35 and having a kid,
I won't be 35 and smiling,
I won't be 35 and with a partner,
I won't be 35 and a teacher,
I won't be 35 and a dancer,
I won't be 35 and a warrior.
I won't be 35.

I need to be free before I can properly survive.
I had to cover myself in red paint,
To honor the parts of me that did not survive.
Time waits for no one they say.
Who said time had to wait?

Who said we should work until we have
nothing?
I am 16 now.
I am a kid.
I am feeling as if I am grown.
I am already 35.

I won't be here much longer if this continues.
I crave little red lines etched into my skin,

Scars of a battle not won or lost.
To explain why I can't have my family,
My life.

At least with the little red lines,
I would be free.
Pour gasoline over my skin,
Burn me as a witch if you can.

I'll die anyway.
No more stories or poems,
Prose gone in woes.
I wish that I never did.

Burn me at the stake like my fallen sisters,

Burned and son of the burned.
I am not a toy,
So why do I feel like I would be plastic?

I have things I don't want.
My body is not mine,
I have no rights under the law,
Why do I have to be 35?
Mama, I won't make it this time.

Covered in paint,
Covered in blood,
Covered in scars,

Covered in burns.
I'll make sure time waits for you,
You are everything I wanted,
Everything I had.

You are the reason I am smiling now,
I will so soon die than let time kill me,
You will take me home in another life,
One by one.
We will be it all.

Time means nothing to the dead,
Time means nothing to the truly living.
Time means everything to me.

Nonverbal

Gifts for the doormat,

"You are quiet today,"

Pull the last bone from the witches' cave,

"Why did you stop talking?"

The rising fear and pain,

"Hey, finish your presentation."

Scratching at the voice box,

"Focus, please."

All the words in my head that won't come out,

"Hey, are you okay?"

Questions I wish I could answer without a doubt.

"Are you suicidal?"

Of course I am,

Why would I live like this?

"Come on, he just asked you out, Respond!"

"Take a hit. You'll feel better."

"Come on drink, live a little!"

"Are you sure it's okay to do this?"

Questions I can no longer answer,

No longer answer because I'm scared.

My voice temporarily locked in a cage,

Pages on pages of words,

"Princess, is this okay?"

"Fucking damn- hottie with an ass!"

I can't say no,

I can't say yes,

Nothing can get out because I'm stuck,

I'm tired and unable to move.

"The woods? That's a quiet place."

"Wanna meet in the library?"

"Kiddo, look at me, follow me."

"Shhh. This is normal."

Nonverbal tendencies amplified by fear,

Frozen so I won't be hurt,

Nonverbal,

Non verbal.

No voice.

No voice.

No choice.

I am not myself sometimes.

I wish I could speak to them this way,

I wish someone would understand.

But I don't have my voice right now,

I'm Nonverbal.

Year by Year

Upon the baby they set their eyes,
Nothing to express within their skies.

Hospital, hospital, another thing to catch,
The poor baby, it just hatched.

Spiders in the corner of the room,
Stare the baby to sleep, pouring out the gloom.

Lady lady! Oh the fight,
I hope the baby doesn't remember this night.

Medusa, Medusa, why did you bring a plight!
The child can barely take flight.

No, no! Mother walked right past an open door,
I don't want the child to remember, get it to the
floor.

Bloody messes along the bathroom wall,
Hidden knives and ace wrap with hidden calls.

Not much more to say, but the kid needs to be
brave,
It always thinks of ways to escape the crave.

A device of control, meant to protect given as a
gift,
It is spoiled and ungrateful for ours. Why does
this shift?

Year 10, year of peace… no… He ruined the
moment for its rage.
Lilith, Lilith, shows the child what it needs to
cope with its cage.

It's angry again… how do we fix this? He needs
help.
Though we watch his movements, he never says
"oh, well".

He has braved it, I fear we may have pushed him
far,
You see, even he has started to see every
damaged scar.

Golden Year! Oh, our little human has grown so
much, though his fear,
He's misplaced it. It is never his fault, he shall
know his own year.

Man has hurt this poor soul,
He cries and cries for months at a time to all
denial of his role.

Third time, when will he realize, he needs to
learn to speak,
Through any medium he will know his wild
streak.

He knows his word as well as he listens to ours,
he must learn his voice,
Lady, Lady show his way, keep him in his tray,
let him learn to rejoice!

Wax Dolls

Made of melted fats,
Formed to be perfect by age.
Reduced by numbers and talent,
Forced to play a dance.
Broken by 11,
Afraid of every word.
Doll,
That's what I was called,
When I was made of plastic stones
When I was made of collard groans.
Now I am filled with wax,
In between the broken cracks,
Trying to form a body that isn't mine.
A doll
A doll
A doll
Is that all I'll ever be?
Wax dolls melt in the sun,
Just as fast as I burn.
Now I am just another statistic,
Just another number,

Just another case.
Just a doll made of wax.

Little Red Lines

I covered my arms,

Looking at the little red lines,

The little red lines,

Drawn in with a pair of scissors.

I promised myself I would never cross those
lines,

Never again,

The little red lines that guide my fate,

Little red reasons.

Every line,

Another reason is that

Drawn in an irreversible ink,

They faded from the sun.

I promised myself I would listen to a no,

I promised I would never do this,

I promised we were just friends,

Then I remembered the little red lines.

Red lines,

Red lines,

Red lines,

No.

I won't make any more,

No more red lines,

No more crossing over promises,

No more red lines.

It has been one hundred ninety days,

No red lines,

No stop signs,

Nothing of note.

But today,

I want to make little red lines,

I wanted to cross a red boundary,

I wanted to betray the bathroom circle.

I promised I wouldn't do it,

Why do I want to?

No more little red lines,

I need to make little red lines

... I'm sorry,

I made a mess,

There are 45 little red lines.

Letters to My Mother

We are not on the same page,

We probably never will be,

You stand beyond me,

Treating me as I act.

I understand I was wrong,

But so are you,

You don't think about the consequences,

Certain actions create the broken feeling.

Chaos we both crave,

But neither pure,

One wrong roll,

And I experience grief again.

I am attached to things that aren't real,

You say they aren't,

That I shouldn't feel this way,

I know.

I shouldn't grieve over something fiction,

But I do,

They're more friendly than you sometimes,

They are real to me.

My trauma feels fake compared to what I've
read,

Stories make me feel like a liar,

Yet I know these characters more than I know
you,

We are not on the same wavelength.

Why do I have to ask you for help,

If I'm clearly drowning,

Do I have to scream when you hear me whisper,

Do I have to lie to you?

My mother,

My mother,

Am I really your son?

Or just another way for you to cope.

My mother,

My mother,

Am I real?

Or just another story you told.

Mother,

Mother,

Do I have to let you go?

When all I ever wanted was to understand?

You say I'm being mean,

I agree,

But then you ask me why,

And then you assume it's because of Eve.

Why can't you see that I'm drowning?

Mother?

Why can't you listen?

Why am I screaming on deaf ears?

You say you know,

You then say you are my friend,

But you're never my mother when I need you.

Always, just a friend,

Repeating my words to you.

Am I just a friend?

Or am I your son?

We can't have both.

I miss you,

We are not growing together,

We're growing apart,

Distant.

Mother,

Are we slowly dying?

Am I the problem?

Is it really my fault if I don't understand?

Mother,

Mother,

Do I have to let you go?

I don't want to let go...

Ichor

I stood before your grace,

Aware of my betrayal,

I never asked your permission or your blessing,

A kneel before you,

Queen of the Gods.

I kneel before your power,

Begging for forgiveness in the betrayal of man,

I never planned for it to be of pain,

I bow before you,

My Lady of Marriage.

I bow to your vengeance,

Calling out your name,

I never planned to ask you to punish me,

I lay before you,

Queen of Olympus.

I look to your eyes,

Down dripped the golden blood,

I never wanted you to cry,

I kneel before you,

My mother Hera.

I feel the heavy drops of Ichor falling down my skin,

Everything stopped in the moment,

I never meant to do this to your grace,

I stand before you today begging for forgiveness,

My Lady.

Derealization

You catch yourself saying things,
'The wind is beautiful in this town',
'Why does this biome breathe with violets',
'You can only find dragons in the mountains'
'Minerals for this sword cost so much.'
'Time is just an illusion that helps things make
sense.'

These things are drawn from a world inside the
admirable work of a creator,
Ones who are meant to create for life.
Hallucinatory visions that bring joy to the blind,
Noises the deaf can hear,
And give the mute words to speak volumes
higher than any politician.
I would rather see the sensibility in someone
with the help of melodies.

Stories are how we decorate emotions, songs are
how we decorate time,
Paintings are how we decorate space.
The world doesn't need decoration, until you
look at us.
Melodies for the dancers, Voices for the writers,
Artists to their own.

Modern-day bards that bring stories to life with
hidden chords.
The pen is only mightier than the sword if the
hand knows what it does.

You now only feel the pixels decorating your
skin,
You only feel the paper cuts, trees revenge.
All for the suffocation of the reality we have
created,
Star-Crossed lovers breathe life into every word
that is uttered under oath,
The largest taught book can only be banned
within the fear of children learning to live.
Reality no longer exists, it's just you and the
creation of another soul.

No Little Red Lines

Red Lines used to cross my arms,
Ribbons of dried blood seeped into my skin,
All I know are the boundaries I have set,
Though I still crave the little red lines,
I'm free for so long,
February holds the year.

I know that there is more than one type of line.
Red being at the top,
Once, I learned not to grab what isn't mine.
Little Red Lines still dot my vision,
Hold my thighs,
And sometimes I even have to hide.

But at least for now...
No Little Red lines....
No Little Red Lines.
I gifted up my world,
Now I see the other colors,
Purple and yellow versions of safety.

I no longer have little red lines,
I am safe and sound without them,
So I now wish them goodbye,
Little Red lines.

Soul Ties

Souls are magma cold,
Full of every hold,
Memories of water and the moon,
All trapped within the sun.

Souls of ice burn,
Connected with every sprinkle,
Changed with the wind and pulled with the sky,
Gods of fate and life,
Stories of untold lives,
Unwritten and unbound by mortal cause,
Together with a bond.

Three connected follows,
Senses of the blood,
Though time changes and pulls,
Follow the Roman rules
Bound by light and radiance,
Follow the sun and the moon,
The star is searching out of place,
Connected with the light.

Souls are tied to one another,
Since the universe formed,
Each concept and overlap,
From wine to dine.

The soul is a ball of string,
Connected to many mates and halves,
Prices of the past.

Follow your heart to the one who knows.
Gifted into your life,
You were made in the same place and time,
You are an oracle.

I Don't Hate You

I hate you.

Everything about you makes me want to die.

I hate what you stand for.

I hate what you work towards.

I hate how unhappy you make me.

So I'll destroy you.

I'll let your blood fall to the ground.

I'll use it to dye my hair.

I'll use it to break out my skin.

I'll use it to cause a fever.

I hate you,

so everything I do will be against you.

Taking away food and colors,

Forcing you to sit still,

Making your interests incomprehensible.

I hate your skin,

Your shape,

Your freckles that look like galaxies,

I hate how you look good in red and blue,

Your eyes and how they remind me of fireflies,

Your smile.

Do I actually hate you?

Do I hate you?

Or do I just hate your stances?

Do I just hate one aspect of you?

Do I hate the world surrounding your light?

Or do I just wish I was like you?

I don't think I actually hate you.

I don't hate your stance.

I don't hate your scars.

I don't hate your eyes,

I don't hate your smile.

Or maybe I do.

I think I just miss the way you were,

Before you became angry,

Before you were hurt.

And afraid.

I missed our silly conversations.

About dinosaurs and chickens,

About the stars,

About the little stories in your head.

I miss your childhood.

I never actually hated you.

I hated that you were hurt.

I hated that you were afraid.

I don't hate you.

I don't hate you.

I don't hate you.

I don't hate you.

But I can't love you yet.

Everything at once

They say nothing heals the past like time,
And that you are born to find your mind,
They force you into everything,
Your world is collapsing before you.

Blood is dripping down the impalement of
pencils,
It won't wash out of the white,
I'm in the trees,
In the breeze,
But I would not let them catch me now.

Running with wolves,
Away from predators of elder ages,
Dancing in the rain,
I wish this was the life I had.

Instead, I'm cutting in my room,
I wish I was dead.

I wish that nothing mattered.
I wish I was aborted.

But I can't let them catch me now.
I am free here,
Safe here,

As I am told,
Be the perfect oldest daughter,
House-wife in training.

Walking with blood dripping from every limb,
Dragging myself up a rocky mountain,
Making myself breathe and run,
My face reflected in places unknown,
I am one with the wind.

Stacks of pages,
Grabbed in cages,
Wrapped in wires,
I'm running away from problems,
Hoping to drown in my own blood,
My heirs' blood at that,
But I can't let them catch me now.

Everything is too much.

Work on work,
Forced into play,
Sex,
Blood
Prison,
And yet it is still my fault.

It is always my fault.

Last night,
One in the morning,
I had a dream of mourners ground,
Whispering prayers to Elysium,
To heaven,
To Midgard.

Praying that their death was swift,
I know it's all in my head,
I see the blood on the dim-lighted floor,
Linoleum floors of an elementary game,
It's Everything at once.

Please do not let them catch me now,
I don't want to be everyone at once,
I do not want to be Everything at once,

I will run,
I will be free.
They won't catch me now.

Lady Medusa

Lady Medusa came to me,

In the eyes of a snake.

She whispers her warning under a hiss.

I paid her no mind,

The stories I've heard,

Were not of her own,

But of the perpetrators.

I pretended not to hear her voice,

Until the fateful night,

I heard her scream.

That's when I knew the story was a lie.

Her myths surround me like a cyclone,

Protective and motherly,

That night,

I heard her cry over me.

Her hiss burns my ears,

A warning I will not so soon forget,

Listening to the elder warnings,

A spiral of emotional distress.

I follow in Lady Medusa's steps,

I follow her warnings,

Her prophecies,

Her stories.

Lady Medusa deserved better,

And so do I.